THE SOUTH DEVON RAILWAY

DON BISHOP

HALSGROVE

First published in Great Britain in 2009

British Library Cataloguing-in-Publication Data
A CIP record for this title is available from the British Library

ISBN 978 1 84114 919 6

HALSGROVE
Halsgrove House,
Ryelands Industrial Estate,
Bagley Road, Wellington, Somerset TA21 9PZ
Tel: 01823 653777   Fax: 01823 216796
email: sales@halsgrove.com

Part of the Halsgrove group of companies
Information on all Halsgrove titles is available at: www.halsgrove.com

Printed and bound by Grafiche Flaminia, Italy

INTRODUCTION

The South Devon Railway is perhaps today the best recreation that there can be of the classic Great Western branch line in the West Country. It exudes a simple quiet atmosphere of times past, unhurried and relaxed. It runs for 7 miles alongside the beautiful River Dart between Buckfastleigh and Totnes. Originally the line ran a further 2 miles to Ashburton, opening on 1 May 1872 as the Buckfastleigh, Totnes and South Devon Railway. This independent railway was built to the broad gauge 7ft ¼ inch, as promoted by Isambard Kingdom Brunel. Although independent the line was operated by the South Devon Railway until February 1876, when the whole SDR system was operated by and later absorbed by the Great Western Railway, including the independent Ashburton branch. The line was converted to the "narrow" (standard) gauge 4ft 8½ inch in May 1892.

The line settled down into its quiet branch line life, with local passenger services running from the junction station at Totnes and goods services often running through from Newton Abbot each day. Competition from bus services between Torquay, Newton Abbot and Ashburton began in the 1920s and passenger traffic started to decline, although the GWR introduced auto train services in 1927 with an improved timetable to try and combat this. Private car ownership also started to have an impact in the 1930s and passenger numbers continued to decline. However petrol rationing during the Second World War period resulted in a reduction in local bus services and private car usage, so the railway enjoyed a revival in the numbers of passengers carried. However this quickly turned back after the end of the war and decline once again set in. Timetable improvements again took place under the newly nationalised British Railways in 1950 to cater for additional usage being made by workers in Staverton and Totnes. However as the overall railway system started to run into the red this level of service could no longer be justified and cuts again took place in 1956. The end of the passenger service came about on 1 November 1958. The line became goods only, although some excursions and schools' specials did operate after this date. A daily goods service operated from Newton Abbot until 1961 when it was changed to run from and return to Plymouth. Final closure to all traffic came on 10 September 1962.

The line was left in situ as talks proceeded on a preservation bid and work to restore the line, which had been taken back by nature in the meantime, was started in 1965. However the Ministry of Transport wanted to use the trackbed between Buckfastleigh and Ashburton for the new A38 dual carriageway road, so this section of the line could not be reopened to passengers. The line to Ashburton was used by the new Dart Valley Railway company in the early days, and indeed the locomotive facilities were located there initially, and some members-only trains were run with special permission, the final special running on 2 October 1971, until the line was truncated at Buckfastleigh. Sadly the lovely terminus station at Ashburton was cut off from the rail network and today survives as part of a garage, with the goods shed and engine shed also still in situ for alternative uses.

The line between Totnes and Buckfastleigh was reopened as the Dart Valley Railway on 5 April 1969 with an "official reopening" on 21 May 1969 by Dr Richard Beeching who had been chairman of the British Transport Commission at the time of the line's closure.

Another problem for the new railway company was that the private railway's trains were unable to enter the mainline station at Totnes, although this did occur for a short time in the mid 1980s until it became too costly to continue that part of the operation. The Dart Valley Railway had to develop their own station at Totnes Riverside, later to become Totnes Littlehempston; however this had no direct access to the town or mainline station until a new footbridge was erected at a later date.

New facilities to run the railway were developed at Buckfastleigh to restore and maintain locomotives, carriages and wagons etc. for use on the line. The line was operated by a mix of volunteers and full time paid staff.

In October 1972 the Dart Valley Railway company also took over operation of the very scenic Paignton–Kingswear line from BR, unusually the line did not actually close and local diesel services continued to operate until 1973 when subsidies for the service were reduced. The new line established itself as the flagship of the Dart Valley Railway Company, carrying far greater passenger numbers than the Buckfastleigh line due to it running right along the popular Torbay coast.

Through the 1980s the Buckfastleigh line continued to operate its heritage steam services, somewhat in the shadows of its "sister" line at Paignton. But costs continued to rise and the Dart Valley Railway company started to discuss what to do in the future and even contemplated closing the line once again. Fortunately the charitable volunteer-led South Devon Railway Trust was formed to take over the line from the Dart Valley Company and this took place in 1991 to become today's separate South Devon Railway.

Since that time the railway has grown from strength to strength with separate bodies formed to oversee running the railway, providing volunteer staff and support, managing retail sales and the locomotive works.

The line has now without doubt become a classic in its own right, with Great Western locomotives and rolling stock working daily services through much of the year. The line carries around 100,000 passengers per year and in 2007 won the prestigious Heritage Railway of the Year award. In 2009 the line celebrates its 40th anniversary as a preserved heritage railway and a big gala event is planned at the time of writing this introduction and images from the event are included within the book.

The book itself aims to show how the South Devon Railway has recreated the typical West Country branch line scene, and to that end a number of the pictures feature the classic autotrain type workings that were for so long a feature of the Ashburton and many other GWR branch lines. There is also a slight BR era bias in the images as that is the period I feel is more accurately able to be recreated in the early twenty-first century. Although the SDR also operates diesel hauled services and special diesel running days these are not included in this book which aims to show the line recreating the classic steam age branch line.

Most of the images are of trains in the landscape, showing how well the line fits into the landscape alongside the River Dart, which it follows nearby for almost its entire length. My photographic season is mainly between the months of October and April when the sun is lower in the sky giving much more pleasant lighting effects to the pictures and the cooler temperatures allow the locomotive exhausts to be visible.

If you decide to try your hand at some steam railway photography yourself please do bear in mind that trespass on the railway's property is not only illegal but can be dangerous and should only be attempted when you have a valid lineside pass and some knowledge and training in railway safety. Please also respect local landowners and do not trespass on adjoining land without permission.

For full details of the railway's timetables and special events visit the website at www.southdevonrailway.co.uk

Dedication. This book is dedicated to all the hard working volunteers and staff of the South Devon Railway and in particular the line's General Manager, Richard Elliott until April 2009, whose unstinting efforts have recreated the wonderful GWR branch line atmosphere we are able to enjoy into the twenty-first century. Thank you.

The line's own 57xx Pannier No. 5786 passing through Staverton Woods with a BR era goods train on 21 April 2009.

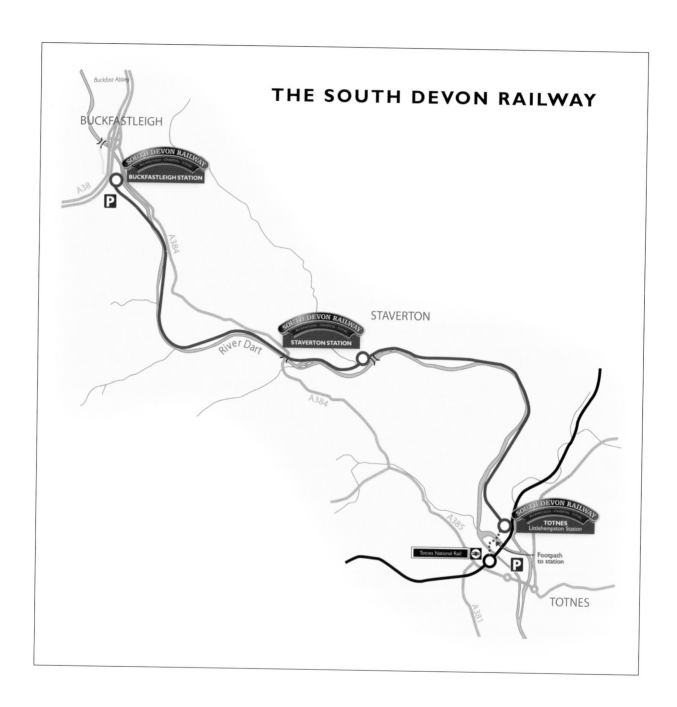

THE SOUTH DEVON RAILWAY

ALONGSIDE THE RIVER

14xx tank No. 1420 propels a single autocoach towards Buckfastleigh at Dartington in spring 1999.

This scene evokes memories of the many milk trains that ran on branch lines in the West Country and then joined up to form express milk services to London. Here 14xx No. 1427 (actually 1420 in disguise) passes Stretchford with two milk tanks and a brake van on a photo charter in March 2000.

Visiting Bodmin Railway-based Pannier No. 6435 passing Stretchford,
South Devon Railway with a Totnes-bound service on 11 April 2009.

A similar view of another Bodmin Railway-based engine visiting the line, this time Prairie No. 5552 running alongside the River at Stretchford with BR red/cream liveried train on 8 April 2009.

Collett 14xx 0-4-2T No. 1450 with a short goods working alongside the Dart at Woodville on 25 April 1997.

During the railway's 40th anniversary event Small Prairie No. 5542 heads an autotrain away towards Totnes at Dartington. 11 April 2009.

BR liveried Prairie pair Nos. 5526 and 5552 passing alongside the river at Stretchford on 12 April 2009.

Left
A rather dull morning greets Prairie No. 5526 as it heads a single Collett coach alongside the river at Hood Bridge forming an early morning Totnes to Buckfastleigh service on 24 March 2008.

Above
GWR Prairie No. 5542 drifting towards Hood Bridge with a
Totnes-bound train on 8 April 2009.

Left:
14xx No. 1450 hauls a short goods along the banks of the River Dart near Hood Bridge on 25 April 1997.

Right,top:
Dramatic lighting catches Small Prairie No. 5542 as it heads a train towards Totnes at Woodville on 11 April 2009.

Right, bottom:
Home-based Prairie No. 5526 with a photo charter branch line train passing near Hood Bridge on 24 April 2004.

BUCKFASTLEIGH

The station forecourt at Buckfastleigh is very nicely presented with a small gathering of vintage cars outside to help complete the scene. It's this attention to detail which is so well carried out at the South Devon Railway.

Above:
14xx No. 1420 propels its single autocoach into Buckfastleigh Station on the evening of 14 March 1999.

Left:
Pannier No. 5756, owned by a group of enthusiasts known as the Worcester Locomotive Society,
arrives at its current home – Buckfastleigh – on 10 April 2007.

No. 5526 shunts stock ready for the morning's departure at Buckfastleigh on 25 April 2004.

BR Black Pannier No. 5786 standing
in Buckfastleigh Station amid all the
usual country station furniture on
22 April 2009.

Above:
A damp and atmospheric morning at Buckfastleigh as an autotrain waits to depart for Totnes.

Right:
BR Black Pannier No. 5786 standing in Buckfastleigh Station whilst on a photo charter on 22 April 2009. A classic West Country branch line station scene.

NURSERY POOL

Sadly the developments required to allow heavier locomotives to use the South Devon line meant losing the appearance of the very pretty river bridge at Nursery Pool. The Great Western Society's Collett 0-4-2T No. 1466 crosses the bridge with two box vans and a brake forming a pick up goods in October 1995.

West Somerset Railway Association-owned Prairie No. 4561, on loan to the SDR in 1998, approaches the bridge with a photo charter recreation of the Ashburton branch goods on 1 May 1998.

Above:
Visiting Prairie No. 4561 steams across the bridge just as it had done countless times before when it worked the Newton Abbot to Ashburton branch goods in BR days, a wonderful recreation of what had been some 40 years earlier. 2 April 1998.

Right:
The fireman on board No. 1466 looks out as it runs onto the bridge with an autocoach on 19 October 1995.

The sheer beauty of the location can be realised as No. 4561 crosses the River Dart at Nursery Pool Bridge with a branch goods a charter on May 1 1998. There was a similar bridge at the north end of Buckfastleigh prior to the building of the A38 dual carriageway road.

The Ashburton branch local is recreated using Collett 14xx tank No. 1420 and carmine autotrailer No. W225, seen slowly crossing Nursery Pool Bridge and the fast running River Dart on the morning of 14 March 1999.

The Local Prairie - 5526

Just after passing under the A384 road bridge known as Hood Bridge at Riverford No. 5526 heads a single Collett coach towards Staverton on 24 March 2008.

Above:
Prairie No. 5526 waiting to leave Buckfastleigh on 1 November 2008.

Left:
The South Devon Railway completed the restoration of Small Prairie No. 5526 on behalf of the owning group and the engine is now based on the line. Here the BR Black-liveried engine heads a local train through Bishops Bridge on the evening of 24 March 2004.

Above:
Small Prairie tanks were once a common sight throughout Devon and Cornwall on branch line trains. Home-based Prairie tank No. 5526 recreates a typical daily scene while working a photo charter round Caddaford curve on 24 April 2004. Some digital manipulation has removed the markings on the A384 road to help create a timeless scene.

Right:
A vintage Ford Popular car owned by the line's General Manager Richard Elliott is parked alongside the road as Richard watches No. 5526 pass by with a train bound for Totnes on 25 April 2004.

Another view of Prairie No. 5526 on the photo charter of 24 April 2004, this time leaving Buckfastleigh in sunny conditions with its late afternoon run to Totnes.

A two coach local train formed for a photo charter on 25 April 2004 passes Caddaford behind No. 5526. The mix of BR Black livery and GWR choc/cream often occurred in the early '50s as locos and stock were gradually repainted from GWR to BR colours.

PANNIER STALWARTS

Pannier No. 6412 was an early stalwart of the Dart Valley line, and indeed worked opening day trains, but it was later sold to the West Somerset Railway Association for use on the Minehead line. However events turned full circle in 2008 when the little Pannier had become too small for further use on the WSR line so was resold back to today's South Devon Railway, where after overhaul it will return to hauling trains on its old haunt. Here the engine passes through the lush greens of summer at Stretchford on 28 May 2006 when making a visit to the line.

Pannier No. 5786 has carried GWR livery for most of its preservation career. On 17 April 2006 it passes alongside the river at Dartington with a Totnes-bound train.

More recently No. 5786 was repainted into BR Black livery and turned to face Totnes, seen here running alongside the river at Dartington from a different viewpoint on 5 April 2009.

The BR Black Pannier matches well with the line's also recently repainted pair of ex-GWR Collett coaches in BR red/cream livery to recreate a typical 1950s' scene. The engine passes along the straight towards Caddaford with a photo charter on 22 April 2009.

The black 57xx Pannier passes along Stretchford straight on 12 April 2009 with a Totnes-bound train.

Another of the small 64xx Panniers that was originally preserved by the Dart Valley Railway returned to the line in spring 2009 for the 40th anniversary celebrations. Now Bodmin Railway-based, Pannier No. 6435 leaves Staverton with a train bound for Totnes on 7 April 2009.

CAPTURING THE GLINT

An irresistible glint, although there is a lineside cable in the way. The glint effect and reflection are just too good to ignore. No. 1420 heads past a flood in a field near Nappers Crossing with a milk train in March 2000.

A golden glint is perhaps a "holy grail" to steam photographers. Here a strong back-lit glint occurs from the setting sun as 14xx tank No. 1420 hauls an evening autotrain charter alongside the river at Woodville on 23 June 1999.

Further magical evening glints as an autocoach is propelled towards Buckfastleigh
by visiting 14xx No. 1466 at Riverford in October 1995.

CADDAFORD

A popular location for photographers on the line is at Caddaford curve. Here 14xx recreation No. 1427 (in reality No. 1420), a once regular Ashburton branch engine, heads past Buckfastleigh's down distant signal at Caddaford with a short milk train in March 2000.

A further view of No. 5526 passing the scenic location at Caddaford with its photo charter on 24 April 2004.

The Small Prairie approaches Caddaford with its short photo charter train on 24 April 2004. Note the high railings of the "new" Nursery Pool Bridge visible in the background.

A classic West Country branch line scene from the past of a goods train ambling through the countryside. Dean Forest Railway-based Prairie No. 5541 working a goods round Caddaford curve on 19 October 1995 whilst paying a short visit to the line.

STRETCHFORD

Above:
In early spring the light is able to get through the trees alongside the line at Stretchford and provide some lovely "dappled light" effects. Here a milk train heads through the woods in March 2000 behind 14xx No. 1427 (actually 1420 in disguise).

Left:
One of the most scenic locations along the line is the area known as Stretchford where views alongside the track and across the River Dart can be obtained. Here an autotrain heads away towards Totnes behind No. 1420 on 13 March 1999.

Didcot Railway Centre-based 0-4-2T No. 1466 heads a short pick up goods past the foot crossing at Stretchford on 19 October 1995.

A powerful shot of GW Collett 2-8-0 No. 3803 passing along the banks of the
Dart at Stretchford heading for Buckfastleigh on 12 April 2009.

Another view of the big 2-8-0 on the same day, 12 April 2009, emerging from the trees at Stretchford heading for Buckfastleigh.

West Somerset-owned BR Black Prairie tank No. 4561 heading past the fresh spring colours
at Stretchford with a recreation of the branch goods on 1 May 1998.

Another BR Black Prairie tank, this time a larger sloping top tank 55xx version,
No. 5526 heads for Totnes alongside the river at Stretchford on 24 March 2008.

No. 5526 heads its photo charter along the long straight at Stretchford on 24 March 2008.

The private 5542 Locomotive Group's Small Prairie No. 5542 was restored for use on the West Somerset line. However in recent years it has spent most of its time working on other preserved lines and often spends time at the South Devon Railway. Here it heads an autotrain through Stretchford on 12 April 2009.

During the 40th anniversary events Bodmin Railway-based Prairie No. 5552 is running through the trees at Stretchford woods with a Totnes-bound train on 12 April 2009. The engine had undergone repairs at Buckfastleigh during the winter enabling it to take part in the gala.

Above:
Visiting Bodmin Railway-based Pannier No. 6435 passing Stretchford with a BR red/cream rake of stock on 7 April 2009.

Left:
Home-based pair, Pannier No. 5786 and Prairie No. 5526 heading past Stretchford on 12 April 2009.

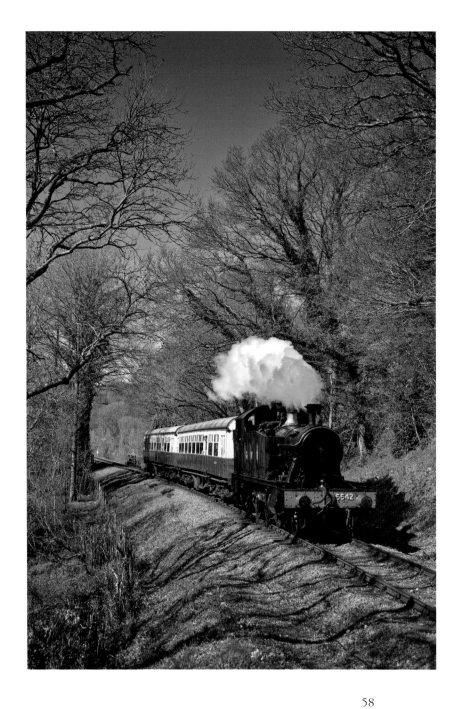

Small Prairie No. 5542 makes a further run along the line with the two autocoaches and passes through the woods at Stretchford on 12 April 2009.

Another visitor to the line in early 2009 was Swanage Railway-based 0-6-2T No. 6695 heading a goods train past Stretchford on 8 April 2009. This engine became the first "red" route engine to work on the line following the upgrading of the axle load limits. Red route engines had previously always been too heavy to work on the line.

4561 AND THE ASHBURTON GOODS

West Somerset Railway Association-owned small Prairie No. 4561 spent the 1998 season on hire to the SDR. Here it heads a goods charter alongside the Dart near Hood Bridge in April 1998.

The Small Prairie was painted BR Black for the last year of its 10 year ticket for the visit to the South Devon Railway. It is seen here crossing Nursery Pool Bridge with a goods train on May 1 1998.

45xx tank No. 4561 had once been a regular engine on the daily goods train from Newton Abbot to Ashburton in the 1950s. Its visit to the SDR in 1998 presented the chance to recreate those scenes and here it runs off of Nursery Pool Bridge towards Buckfastleigh with a goods train on 3 April 1998.

A branch goods is taken towards Buckfastleigh at Stretchford by 45xx No. 4561 on 3 April 1998.

The peace and quiet of the riverside is briefly disturbed by 45xx tank No. 4561 running alongside the river at Dartington with its charter goods recreation on 3 April 1998.

A personal favourite view of the Nursery Pool Bridge before it was modified was this angle along the river from the east side. The 45xx tank crosses the bridge heading for Buckfastleigh with a goods on 1 May 1998.

The West Somerset Railway Association-owned 45xx tank No. 4561 was withdrawn for a scheduled overhaul at the end of 1998, a season it spent on hire to the South Devon Railway and was newly repainted in BR Black livery. Here it runs through Stretchford with the "Ashburton goods recreated" charter on 1 May 1998 heading towards Buckfastleigh.

ASHBURTON AUTOS

The Ashburton line only ever had light passenger traffic and so was a regular haunt for the GWR's autotrains. The South Devon Railway has been keen to recreate this for future generations to see and learn about. The SDR's own 14xx Collett tank No. 1420 crosses the Nursery Pool Bridge with a single autotrailer on 14 March 1999.

A classic scene from the Ashburton branch of old as No. 1420 propels a single autocoach down the branch on 14 March 1999.

Above:
A lovely evening glint is caught by 14xx tank No. 1466 hauling autocoach No. W228
round the curve at Riverford.

Right:
An evening special auto working is caught running alongside the river at
Woodville behind No. 1420 on 23 June 1999.

PRAIRIE POWER

The sharp curve at Luscombe witnesses the passing of home-based 55xx tank No. 5526 once again on 24 April 2004 with a local branch line train.

55xx Prairie No. 5542 heads an autotrain through Riverford on 12 April 2009.

Bodmin Railway-based Prairie No. 5552 running bunker first past Stretchford with a
Buckfastleigh-bound train on the evening of 11 April 2009.

The peace is disturbed as Prairie No. 5526 passes Stretchford on 25 April 2004 with a two coach local of GWR liveried stock.

South Devon's own Prairie No. 5526 rounds Caddaford curve on 25 April 2004.

A damp autumn morning at Buckfastleigh as No. 5526 leaves with the red and cream set on 1 November 2008.

The woods at Luscombe start to show more signs of spring as No. 5526 passes through on the morning of 25 April 2004.

Another view of the very successful photo charter on 24 April 2004 with No. 5526 on a two coach + van local train, this time passing the accommodation crossing at Stretchford.

SPRING AUTOS

Two views of SDR based Collett 0-4-2T No. 1420 with a single carmine-liveried autocoach,
here passing the daffodils at Dartington on 14 March 1999.

Above:

Our second spring view at Dartington shows a classic Ashburton branch scene as Collett 0-4-2T No. 1420 heads towards Totnes with its single autocoach on 14 March 1999.

Right:

Home-based small Prairie No. 5526 propels an evening autotrain past Stretchford, on 8 April 2009.

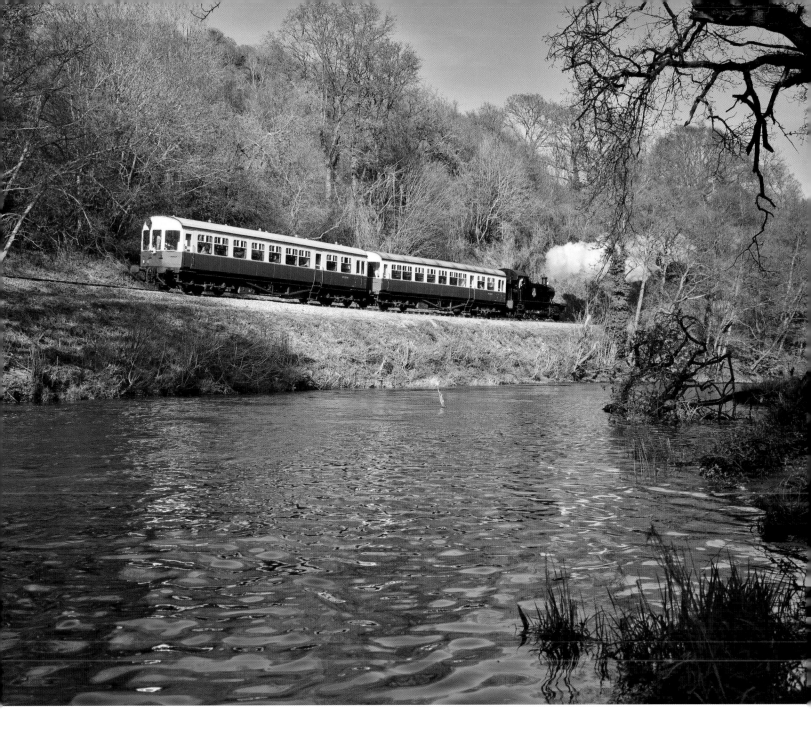

GWR liveried Prairie No. 5542 and autotrain reflect in the River Dart at Dartington just as the sun reappears from behind a cloud on 5 April 2009.

MILK FOR LONDON

Milk trains were once a "staple diet" for many West Country branch lines, indeed a number of lines survived after the infamous Beeching axe purely to cater for milk traffic until this gradually transferred to road haulage through the 1970s. Buckfastleigh's home bracket signal stands guard over the station area as 14xx tank No. 1427 (1420 in disguise for the day) steams slowly out with its short early morning milk train recreation.

Fine autumn lighting and dark clouds greet No. 1427 as it gets away from Buckfastleigh near Nursery Pool Bridge with a typical daily branch milk train to connect with the main-line train to London at the branch junction.

A very tranquil scene as BR Black 0-4-2T No. 1427 (1420 in disguise) slowly crosses Nursery Pool Bridge with its branch milk train in March 2000.

A pair of typically scruffy 6 wheel milk tanks (they were glass lined inside!) is taken round the curve at Caddaford by 14xx tank No. 1427 in March 2000.

The milk train eases around Luscombe curve as its makes its way towards the mainline behind No. 1427 in March 2000.

40 YEARS A HERITAGE LINE

In April 2009 the South Devon Railway celebrated 40 years as a heritage private railway, having re-opened as the Dart Valley Railway in April 1969. A 9 day gala spectacular was staged to mark the event. Over the next few pages we will take a look at some of the locomotives and trains that ran during this celebration of Great Western/BR Western Region branch line steam. It's unusual to see two engines from another heritage line double heading a train away from home – Bodmin Railway-based pair 55xx No. 5552 and 64xx No. 6435 passing Staverton Woods with a Totnes-bound train on 11 April 2009.

Another view of the Bodmin Railway-based Prairie No. 5552, here whistling
and coasting towards the home signal at Hood Bridge on 11 April 2009.

Swanage Railway-based GW 66xx 0-6-2T No. 6695 became the first "red route" loco to work on the line following the raising of the axle load limit. Here it passes Riverford with a goods working to Staverton on 11 April 2009. The GWR used colour codes to indicate the route availability of its engines and in past days only engines with Yellow and Blue classification were able to traverse the Buckfastleigh/Ashburton line.

For the gala the SDR repainted Pannier No. 5786 into BR Black livery and two GWR Collett coaches into the BR 1950s' red and cream livery to recreate a branch line train of that period. I took the opportunity of arranging a photo charter with this combination which is seen here among the Primroses growing alongside the line at Luscombe on 22 April 2009.

Right:
Pannier No. 6435 & GW 0-6-2T No. 6695 head through dappled light at Riverford Woods on 12 April 2009.

Bodmin Railway-based Pannier No. 6435 passing Dartington with a typical two coach BR red/cream branch line train on 7 April 2009.

The Bodmin-based small Prairie No. 5552 running alongside the River Dart at Stretchford with an afternoon goods train to Staverton on 11 April 2009.

The same location witnesses another Bodmin-based engine, Pannier No. 6435, passing the waterfalls on 12 April 2009 with a Totnes-bound train.

A beautiful reflection of GW Collett 2-8-0 No. 3803 as it passes Hood Bridge heading for Buckfastleigh on 11 April 2009.

MORE AUTOTRAINS

The SDR's own 14xx Collett tank No. 1420 heading its single autocoach past Stretchford between Buckfastleigh and Staverton on 13 March 1999.

Another view across the river at Stretchford sees home-based Small Prairie
No. 5526 passing with an autotrain on 8 April 2009.

Before the bridge was modernised in order to allow locomotives with higher axle weights to cross, the bridge over the River Dart at Nursery Pool near Buckfastleigh was a real classic photo location. Here a timeless scene is recreated as 0-4-2T No. 1466, on loan from the Great Western Society at Didcot, propels an autocoach across the bridge amid autumn hues in October 1995.

HOOD BRIDGE

One of the most visible locations of the line to passing motorists is at the narrow traffic-light-controlled Hood Bridge.
Another view of our milk train recreation in March 2000 approaching Hood Bridge behind No. 1427.

An unusual view of the line from under the arches of Hood Bridge, only possible when the river levels are very low. 14xx No. 1450 passes by with a short pick up goods on 25 April 1997.

Early in the morning the light is on the east side of the line just enough to allow a picture of approaching trains with the River Dart in the background. Prairie No. 5526 opens up on getting "the road" from Bishops Bridge Box outer home signal – situated next to the bridge.

A pleasant late afternoon view when the sun has moved round to light the bridge behind for Buckfastleigh-bound trains. Prairie No. 5542 propelling two autocoaches on 12 April 2009.

The Bishops Bridge outer home signal can just be seen in the clear position as
BR Black Pannier No. 5786 approaches Hood Bridge on 22 April 2009.

A view from near lineside level as Bodmin Railway-based Pannier No. 6435 passes with a BR red/cream branch line train on 11 April 2009.

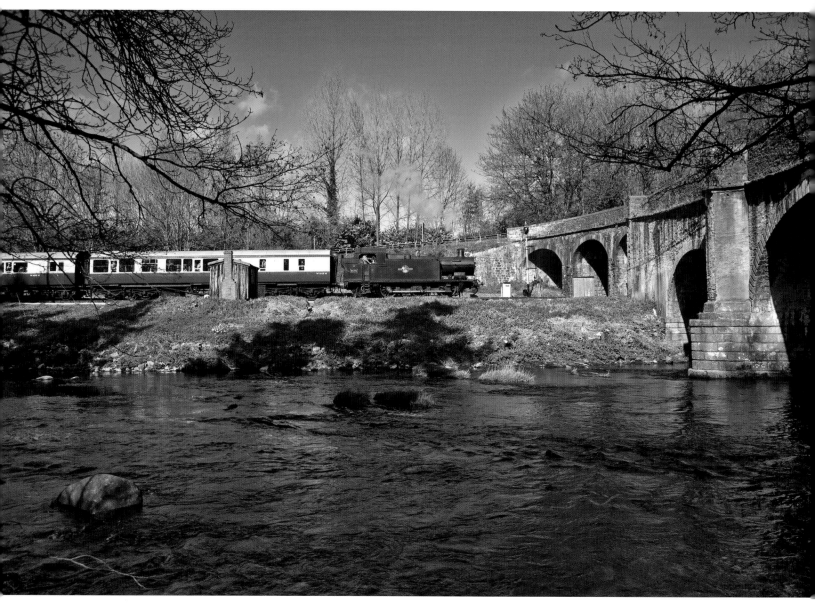

An unusual side-on view of Hood Bridge as 66xx 0-6-2T No. 6695 starts away from the signal on 12 April 2009.

RIVERFORD

As trains continue on their way towards Totnes they pass a location known as Riverford – some maps also refer to the bridge by this name. Small GWR Pannier No. 1369 passes with a single GW coach as a shuttle to Staverton on 11 April 2009.

Although running bunker first I personally love this shot of Bodmin Railway-based Prairie No. 5552 running past Riverford with a single BR red/cream liveried suburban coach on 11 April 2009. Shades of the long lost Princetown branch.

Heading back to Buckfastleigh bunker first is Prairie No. 5542 with the line's two autocoaches – then in different liveries – passing Riverford on 17 April 2006.

Dark clouds brood overhead as GWR Prairie No. 5542 heads past Riverford on 7 April 2009.

5542

No. 5542 comes to stand at Hood Bridge with an autotrain bound for Totnes on 17 April 2006.

Although not always based on the South Devon line, GWR Prairie No. 5542 spends some time each year at Buckfastleigh undergoing maintenance and then runs for a period on the line. Here the engine passes Dartington as seen across the River Dart with a Totnes train on 7 April 2009.

GWR Prairie No. 5542 was initially restored for use on the West Somerset Railway. However, after a few years there was insufficient work for the engine and so it now spends time at various heritage lines around the UK on hire. The engine is seen passing Stretchford with a Totnes-bound train on 8 April 2009.

Autotrain working equipment has been fitted to No. 5542 and here it heads a single autocoach past Stretchford on 11 April 2009.

BISHOPS BRIDGE

The South Devon line's smallest regular engine is Small GWR 0-6-0 Pannier No. 1369, seen here during shunting at Bishops Bridge and Staverton on 11 April 2009.

The SDR's own 14xx Collett tank No. 1420 seen from the signal box steps at Bishops Bridge with an autotrain on the evening of 23 June 1999.

The bracket for Bishops Bridge signal box's up home signals indicates the route ahead for 14xx No. 1427 with a milk train.

A similar view with Collett 0-6-0 No. 3205, now based on the South Devon line, working into Bishops Bridge with a goods on a sunny and clear day in November 1999.

A more distant view of Bishops Bridge is possible from the road leading down into Staverton from the A384. On this occasion No. 4561 is seen heading a short goods train past the loop in April 1998 before the loop was fully commissioned.

During the 40th anniversary events various goods trains were operated. Here Bodmin Railway-based Pannier No. 6435 leaves Bishops Bridge loop with a short engineer's ballast working on 11 April 2009.

STAVERTON

Immediately beyond Bishops Bridge is Staverton Station. These next two images are night scenes with No. 1420 waiting for the porters to return and load the remaining luggage on board. 21 November 1998.

The station master and fireman have a discussion at Staverton Station on the evening of 21 November 1998.

Home-based Small Prairie No. 5526 leaves Staverton and passes the stabling siding with two autocoaches on 8 April 2009. In the background can be seen the railway's Class 37 diesel No. D6737.

Below:
A trolley load of luggage awaits dispatch on the next train at Staverton Station.
A more idyllic branch line scene cannot be imagined.

BR Black Pannier No. 5786 arriving at Staverton Station on 22 April 2009.

14xx Variety

The 14xx 0-4-2 tanks were for many years the staple motive power for the old Ashburton branch and we are very fortunate that four of these little engines survived into preservation, three of which are in working order and have graced the line in recent years. Home-based No. 1420 rounds the sharp curve at Luscombe between Buckfastleigh and Staverton with an auto working on 13 March 1999.

Great Western Society, Didcot-based 14xx 0-4-2T No. 1466 rounding Caddaford curve with a single red and cream autotrailer on 19 October 1995.

Left:
A lovely reflection of No. 1420 and both of the SDR's autotrailers, one in plain carmine and the other in lined maroon, passing a flooded field near Nappers Halt with a service to Totnes in spring 2000.

Another view of the Didcot-based 14xx tank during its 1995 visit to the SDR. A short branch goods is taken slowly across Nursery Pool Bridge behind No. 1466 on 19 October 1995.

Rich autumn colours abound in evening lighting as No. 1420 propels its autocoach into the setting sun near Staverton on 21 November 1998.

The tranquil waters of the River Dart are crossed at Nursery Pool near Buckfastleigh on 13 March 1999 by No. 1420 and a single carmine autocoach. What a simply beautiful scene.

An autotrain passes the gated farm crossing at Stretchford behind No. 1466 on 19 October 1995.

The waters of the River Dart rush alongside as No. 1420 propels autotrailer W225 past Stretchford on 13 March 1999.

Didcot's 14xx tank No. 1466 heads two box vans past Stretchford as a photo charter goods working on 19 October 1995.

BRANCH GOODS

Pannier No. 1369 spent its first 10 year boiler ticket in preservation painted in BR Black livery. Here it passes along the river banks near Hood Bridge with a goods working in the last of the day's light on 19 April 1996.

Dean Forest Railway-based small Prairie No. 5541 visited the line in 1995 and here passes along the straight at Stretchford with a goods in October that year.

Another autumn scene with a Prairie hauled goods, No. 5526 heads away from Buckfastleigh and rounds Caddaford curve with a photo charter on 11 November 2006.

Small GWR Pannier No. 1369 passing Staverton Wood with a single box van and brake from Totnes to Staverton on 11 April 2009.

A branch goods leaves Buckfastleigh behind 55xx tank No. 5526 on 11 November 2006.

It appears that today's goods train is just two box vans! A recreation of a typical Ashburton branch goods with Didcot's 14xx tank No. 1466 heading out of Buckfastleigh on 19 October 1995.

BR Black Pannier No. 5786 leaving Buckfastleigh with a goods train on 21 April 2009,
a typical country branch scene recreated as far as is possible in the twenty-first century.

Collett 0-4-2T No. 1466 with its two box vans works quietly past Woodville on the approaches to Totnes on 19 October 1995.

Left:
Tyseley, Birmingham-based Pannier No. 7760 spent the summer of 1996 on the South Devon Railway and on 11 October 1996 was used on a photo charter recreating a goods from an earlier period using GWR and private owner liveried wagons. It is seen here passing Stretchford.

Below:
The line's own 57xx Pannier No. 5786 passing through Staverton Woods with a BR era goods train on 21 April 2009.

5786

Another image of the line's 57xx Pannier – this time in the earlier GWR livery and facing Buckfastleigh.
The engine passes Riverford with a short GWR set of stock on 17 April 2006.

The repainting of No. 5786 into BR Black has proved popular. On 21 April 2009 the engine passes alongside the A384 road at Caddaford with a photo charter goods train.

Save for the fresh and clean paint work, a perhaps typical branch line goods scene is witnessed as Pannier No. 5786 rounds the curve at Luscombe with a photo charter on 21 April 2009.

One of the most memorable things about this shot was the strong smell of wild garlic – BR Black Pannier No. 5786 passes through Staverton Woods on 22 April 2009.

Another view of the photo charter on the evening of 22 April 2009 – No. 5786 passing Woodville with its two coach local set.

DARTINGTON

Above:

GW Collett 2-8-0 No. 3803 passing along the banks of the Dart at Dartington heading for Buckfastleigh on 11 April 2009. Fairly clear views can be had in early spring from this location, particularly of Buckfastleigh-bound trains.

Right:

A good spot for photography during the late afternoon is across the river from Dartington. On 14 March 1999 14xx 0-4-2T No. 1420 heads alongside the river with an autotrain for Totnes.

GWR Prairie No. 5542 propelling an autotrain past Dartington as seen across the river on 5 April 2009.

TOTNES

The branch goods arrives at Totnes for onward transfer to a mainline train perhaps! Didcot's 14xx tank No. 1466 approaches Totnes Littlehempston on 19 October 1995.

At Totnes the South Devon has its own station known as Totnes Littlehempston, a small village nearby, which is located across a footbridge from the mainline station and town. Pannier No. 5786 stands in Totnes SDR station with a train to Buckfastleigh on 24 August 2008.

Above:
At the end of a successful day's photography on a photo charter Pannier No. 5786 runs round at Totnes and passes the new Ashburton Junction signal box on 22 April 2009.

Right:
Another view of No. 5786 standing at Totnes Station awaiting departure time on 24 August 2008.

THE COLLETT GOODS

Only one member of this once quite numerous class survives. The GWR Collett goods 0-6-0s were built to replace earlier ageing designs both before and after the Second World War, No. 3205 was built in 1946 at Swindon works. Buckfastleigh church stands on the hill behind overlooking the scene as No. 3205 heads away along the branch with its goods on 6 November 1999.

Collett goods 0-6-0 No. 3205 doing what it was designed to do – hauling a short goods along the branch at Caddaford on 6 November 1999. The engine had been temporarily changed to BR unlined green livery by the use of transfers applied with nothing other than Vaseline with the owner's blessing.

Above:
A branch goods ambles alongside the river at Stretchford behind No. 3205 on 6 November 1999. Such scenes were once commonplace on much of the Western Region, in particular these engines worked the highly scenic lines around Gloucestershire and Herefordshire.

Left:
In lovely lighting conditions Collett 0-6-0 No. 3205 passes a flooded field at Nappers with a goods train charter.

THE BIG GOODS

At the other end of the scale in terms of goods engines are the 38xx 2-8-0s. The South Devon Railway Association restored GWR 38xx 2-8-0 No. 3803 over a number of years with completion in 2005. Although strictly speaking too big for the line in typical terms it has proved a popular engine with the crews. As a 2-8-0 design it was also able to work the line in axle weight terms being a Blue route engine, although its long wheelbase is something of a problem on the line's tight curves. The engine is seen approaching Buckfastleigh at Caddaford on 15 April 2008.

Pure Great Western as 38xx 2-8-0 No. 3803 passes alongside the River Dart at Hood Bridge with a Buckfastleigh-bound train on a damp and grey 1 November 2008.

Above:
Doing the kind of work it was designed to do – GW Collett 2-8-0 No. 3803 heads a goods past Riverford heading for Buckfastleigh on 11 April 2009.

Left:
38xx 2-8-0 No. 3803 approaching Staverton on 1 November 2008.

SDR ENGINES AWAY

A welcome side of our steam heritage lines today is the frequent loaning out of engines to attend galas and special events around the country. The South Devon line often lends out engines and in the following few images we see SDR-based engines away from home. Small Pannier No. 1369 has been a popular special events guest at a number of heritage lines around the UK. Here it is seen shunting in the former goods yard at Dunster on the West Somerset Railway on 4 October 2003.

Collett 0-4-2T No. 1420 visited the Severn Valley Railway in March 2001 when painted in fully lined out BR Black livery, like a few class members in the 1950s. On 3 March 2001 it enters Hampton Loade Station whilst numbered as No. 1417 with the SDR's matching autocoach No. W225.

Right:
Not only does the SDR loan out its engines but several railways have also benefited from the loan of the railway's autocoaches. The pairing of the SDR's 14xx tank and autocoach No. W225 is seen at Hampton Loade, Severn Valley Railway in March 2001.

Below:
Another view of No. 1420 masquerading as No. 1417 on the Severn Valley Railway, this time leaving Bewdley Tunnel on 3 March 2001.

Another visit to Severn Valley metals was made in September 2008, this time Prairie No. 5526 and autocoach W225. Here the engine and coach is seen leaving Bewdley SVR on 21 September 2008.

Pannier No. 5786 visited the West Somerset Railway for their 2003 spring gala and on 30 March that year it leaves Blue Anchor along with sister 57xx Pannier No. 5764 from the Severn Valley Railway.